HACKS
FOR
MINECRAFTERS

EARTH

AN **UNOFFICIAL**
HACKERATORS GUIDE

HACKS
FOR
MINECRAFTERS

THE UNOFFICIAL GUIDE TO TIPS
AND TRICKS THAT OTHER GUIDES
WON'T TEACH YOU

TOP SECRET

EARTH

MEGAN MILLER

Sky Pony Press
New York

Sky Pony Press books may be purchased in bulk at special discounts for sales promotion, corporate
gifts, fund-raising, or educational purposes. Special editions can also be created to specifications.
For details, contact the Special Sales Department, Sky Pony Press, 307 West 36th Street, 11th Floor,
New York, NY 10018 or info@skyhorsepublishing.com.

Sky Pony® is a registered trademark of Skyhorse Publishing, Inc.®,
a Delaware corporation.

Minecraft® is a registered trademark of Notch Development AB.
The Minecraft game is copyright © Mojang AB.

Visit our website at www.skyponypress.com.

10 9 8 7 6 5 4 3 2 1

Library of Congress Cataloging-in-Publication Data is available on file.

Cover design by Brian Peterson

Print ISBN: 978-1-5107-6208-4
Ebook ISBN: 978-1-5107-6450-7

Printed in China

TABLE OF
CONTENTS

This guide is based on the early access version of Minecraft Earth, so some features may have been changed, added, or removed between writing this book and publication. Check out the Appendix: More Resources for online resources that cover all of the up-to-the-minute additions to Minecraft Earth.

CHAPTER 1

GETTING STARTED

When you open Minecraft Earth, you'll first see a starting screen for a few moments before the main game screen opens up. The main screen will show you a Minecraft-style map of the streets and paths around you: The world map. The world map will also display icons of tappables (grassy and rocky mounds, trees, animals) and adventure sites that emit beacons of light. As you move around, the map will update to show your new location and any new tappables or adventures.

Minecraft Earth is a mobile, augmented reality (AR) game, which means it uses data from your real-world environment (your device's location, local maps, and camera). It adds tappable and adventure icons to a map of your surroundings, and places adventure and building scenes so that they appear on your mobile device's screen as if they are directly in front of you. To play Minecraft Earth ordinarily, you'll need to be able to walk or move around your neighborhood to find new tappables and adventures. However, Mojang, the game developer, has also experimented with increasing the radius for accessing tappables and added crystal adventures that you can play in your home.

World Map

(A) WORLD MAP
(B) BUILDINGS AND
    STRUCTURES
(C) TAPPABLES
(D) PUBLIC PATHS
(E) STREETS

Installing Minecraft Earth

To play the game, you'll need to install it on your mobile device (tablet or smartphone) first. If your device runs iOS, you can get Minecraft Earth from Apple's App Store, and if you have an Android device, you can download the game from the Google Play Store. Not all devices can support Minecraft Earth, though. Your device needs to support some specific AR-related technologies. Generally, if you have iOS 10 or later and Android 8 or later, you should be fine. Mojang (the developers) have a list of incompatible devices at Help.minecraft.net in the Minecraft Earth Section. Once you have the game installed, you'll also be asked to sign in to your existing Microsoft or Xbox Live account or create a new one. Also, you'll need to accept prompts for giving access to Minecraft Earth for your camera and your location.

There are three main areas of gameplay in Minecraft Earth: collecting, adventuring, and building. You collect resources (wood, plants, stone, etc.) by clicking on tappables in the world map. Afterwards, you can create more objects and items by combining (crafting) them with your crafting table or cooking (smelting) them in your furnace. In adventures, you place a 3D adventure scene into your world, and interact with it to collect more stuff, solve puzzles, and kill the baddies (skeletons, zombies, creepers, etc.). In build mode, you place a 3D buildplate into your world, where you can remove and add blocks and animals to create buildings and scenes.

Playing Immediately

This chapter looks in detail at the user interface of Minecraft Earth, but you don't need to understand every detail to start playing the collecting game. Once your world map shows up, you can walk around and start collecting resources. The game will also guide you through a first few tappables through prompts. Otherwise, look at your circular range indicator, and when tappables (trees, animals, chests, grassy mounds, and rocky mounds) appear within this range, you can tap on them several times to collect their resources. Beacons emitting light are adventures, and you'll probably want to know a little bit more about these before playing one. At the very least, you will want to craft a sword and a pickaxe before playing!

(A) CHEST TAPPABLE
(B) SHEEP TAPPABLE
(C) PIG TAPPABLE
(D) COW TAPPABLE
(E) GRASSY POND
     TAPPABLE
(F) GRASS TAPPABLE
(G) STONE TAPPABLE
(H) CHICKEN TAPPABLE

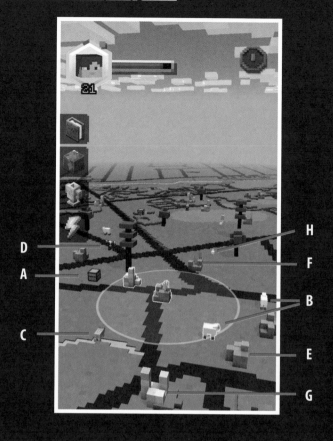

OpenStreetMap
Minecraft Earth uses official open data from OpenStreetMap, which itself is created by a community of users like you. Mojang in fact suggests that if you see a problem with the map of your location, join OpenStreetMap and improve its local mapping.

In addition to the world map, the main screen displays a number of other buttons or links to other features and information: your profile, direction, game challenges, your inventory, the shop, and more.

The world map will show you a 3D view of your current location and it will update as you move around. You can increase the area that the map shows using a pinch gesture (two fingers moving closer together) and zoom back in with a stretch gesture (two fingers moving apart). The circle around your avatar shows which tappables you can click. You can only open those tappables within your radius, and you have to physically move to get near enough to other tappables.

Tappables

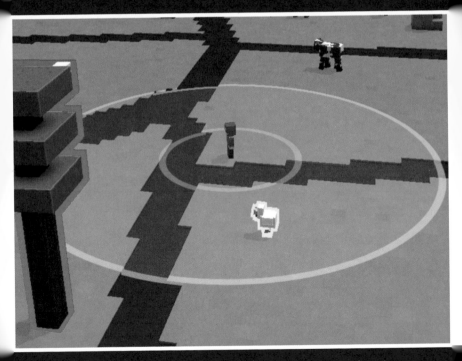

You can only collect tappables that are inside your play circle, or radius. As you move

Compass

When you start playing, the compass needle points straight up, north, and the world map is also positioned so that north is at the top of the map. Your avatar shows you which direction you yourself are facing, according to your device's GPS. You can swipe in a circle on the map to change the map's direction. As the map turns, the compass needle also swings to show you where North is relative to your direction.

If you want the compass and map to set to the same direction that you (as shown by your avatar) are facing, click the compass to link them both (a link icon will show on the compass).

The compass's needle swings to show where North is (top); clicking the compass icon links the compass to the direction your device (and avatar) is facing.

Profile

The profile icon has several different elements to tell you your status in the game. First, the player head represents you and will show your head with the skin (costume) you have chosen. You can change your costume by clicking on the profile icon and selecting new costumes in the character section. See page 9 for more on changing your profile. The health bar on the right will show you how healthy you are—the longer the red line, the better. If the bar is low, you're close to death. You'll need to eat food to regenerate your health. See page 66 for more on your health. The number below the profile icon shows your current experience level. The border around your profile icon shows your progress in yellow toward the next experience level. See page 9 for more on experience.

Player Profile

(A) AVATAR
(B) EXPERIENCE POINTS AT CURRENT LEVEL
(C) NEW ITEMS AVAILABLE IN CHARACTER CREATOR
(D) HEALTH BAR
(E) EXPERIENCE LEVEL

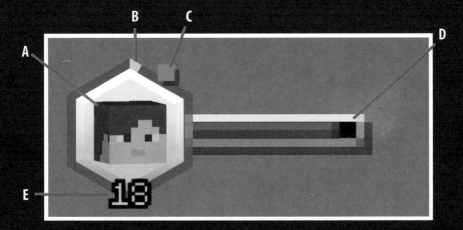

Click your profile's icon to open up your profile's overview, the Character Creator, your stats, and game settings.

Side Menu

The side menu has links to Challenges and Boosts. Challenges are collection and buildplate tasks that you can perform to gain more experience—as you gain more experience, you gain access to new buildplates. Boosts are purchaseable augments to your game—they may increase your range for accessing tappables or double the amount of experience you get for collecting animals. You purchase them through an in-game currency called rubies.

(A) JOURNAL
(B) SEASONAL CHALLENGES
(C) CHALLENGES
(D) BOOSTS

Rubies

Rubies are the in-game currency. You can purchase them directly through the Shop (a minimum purchase of 40 rubies cost $1.99) or you can earn them through gameplay. Rubies are randomly awarded to you when you collect tappables and completing challenges can also grant you a few rubies.

Bottom Menu

The main menu at the bottom has buttons for Inventory, Crystals/Adventures, Make Stuff, Buildplates, and Store. Inventory is where all the goods you collect are stored. The Crystals/Adventures area allows you to load and place Crystal adventures or normal Adventures at your current location. Make Stuff is where you craft and smelt resources to create new goods. In the Store section, you can purchase Rubies for money and then purchase Buildplates and Boosts for Rubies.

A   B   C   D   E

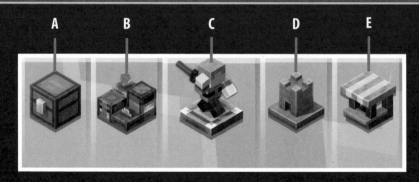

(A) INVENTORY   (C) ADVENTURES   (E) STORE
(B) MAKE STUFF   (D) BUILDPLATES

Changing Your Profile

If you click your profile icon on the World Map, the Profile area will open up. This is where you can customize your game settings, check in on your stats, and change your skin (your character and costume). Click the icons along the top to open the different sections of your profile: Overview, Characters, Activity Log, and Settings.

Profile Overview Screen

In the Overview Screen, you'll see your character, your character's (in-game) name, your experience level, and a progress bar showing how far along you are in reaching the next experience level.

Profile Overview

Experience
As you get higher and higher in levels, the more experience points it takes to get to the next level. For example, it takes 1000 points to get from level 2 to level 3, but 19,000 points to get from level 18 to level 19.

At the bottom of the overview screen you'll see some icons that show your stats. Click on each to see the details of your play from the number of blocks placed to the number of mobs you've defeated.

Settings

In the Settings screen, you'll be able to change a variety of game options as well as report any problems you may be having. You can turn off the vibration that your device might give as alerts (this usually happens when your radius in the World Map encounters new tappables and adventures). Precision mode gives you a crosshair in buildplates and adventures so you can more easily see where you are placing or breaking blocks. Bright mode is a mode designed to make it easier to see the game screens when you are outside in sunlight. Battery Saver will let you pause the game and save battery usage by turning your phone face down. If you turn Touch Input on, the screen will show a bright yellow box whenever and wherever you touch it. Finally, you can click on the language you'd like the game to use. (Sadly, "LOLCAT" is not yet an option as it is in the Java edition.) Below the top settings, you'll find links and information about your game, from reporting bugs and giving feedback to reading the privacy policy.

Sign Out

Several people can use the same device to play. To log out of and into new accounts, click this button here under Settings.

Haptic Vibration

The vibrations you feel with some mobile device applications are produced by haptic technology — technology that gives the sense of touch to a user. In mobile devices, the vibrations are created by a tiny motor.

Activity Log

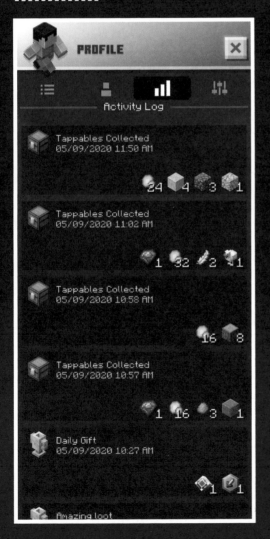

Click the graph button at the top of the Profile area's menu to open your activity log. This documents your daily accomplishments from the loot and experience gained collecting tappables to the challenges you've completed.

Characters

The main menu at the bottom has buttons for Inventory, Crystals/Adventures, Make Stuff, Buildplates, and Store. Inventory is where all the goods you collect are stored. The Crystals/Adventures area allows you to load the money spot of the Profile area, "Characters" (also called the Character Creator), which is where you go to change your skin. Your skin includes the whole look of your character, including height, shape, and costume. None of these costume choices affect gameplay, so even if it looks like you've got a sheath of arrows on your back, in the game, you don't.

Characters Screen

The bottom grid shows stored favorite skins. If you click on the Trash icon, you'll delete the current skin.

In the "Dressing Room" you'll be presented with some featured skin elements. Use the bottom menu to browse purchaseable and free costumes, body elements, and accessories. To access the Character Creator, click the paintbrush icon. Here you can alter the look of your skintone, height, hair color, and eyes, and find the free options for your character.

You can tell these are only available by purchase by the tiny yellow coin with an "m" on it. This is another Minecraft currency called Minecoins that is used in the Minecraft Marketplace, which is affiliated primarily with the Bedrock edition of Minecraft played on consoles and Windows 10.

There are two premade skins for you to choose from in the saved skins area at the bottom of the opening Characters screen. These are the classic "Steve" and "Alex" skins from the original Java edition of Minecraft, but you can click Edit to enter the "Dressing Room" where you can choose from free or buyable skins or skin elements like hats and shoes, and place Crystal adventures or normal Adventures at your current location. Make Stuff is where you craft and smelt resources to create new goods. In the Store section, you can purchase Rubies for money and then purchase Buildplates and Boosts for Rubies.

Dressing Room

A

(A) YOUR MINECOIN ACCOUNT
Click the + button to add more.

(B) FEATURED ELEMENTS
If these have a minecoin icon attached, you'll need to pay!

(C) FEATURED
Featured skin elements to purchase.

(D) CHARACTER CREATOR
Where you want to go to freely customize your avatar.

(E) CLASSIC SKINS
Skin packs that may or may not be free.

CHAPTER 2

STUFF: COLLECTING AND MAKING IT

A huge part of Minecraft Earth is collecting and making stuff, also known as "resources." You'll use these resources to build and make tools, weapons, and food. You'll also be collecting mobs—animals and other creatures you can also store or place on buildplates.

Collecting Tappables

Collecting tappables is simple. Walk around with your phone or mobile device running the game and look at the map. When a tappable icon (a grass mound, a rocky mound, trees, chests, or an animal) comes within your avatar's radius, click several times to open and reveal the resources contained within. The goods will automatically be delivered to your inventory.

Types of Tappables

Different types of tappables will give you different types of resources: grassy mound tappables have plant and earthy resources, and rocky mound tappables will give you items more related to stone and mining. Tapping a tree will give you logs of wood from that tree and sometimes a sapling. Animal tappables bring an animal or its variant and sometimes a related good. For example, a chicken tappable will bring you a chicken or its chicken variant, the cluckshroom, and sometimes a feather. Chests usually contain crafted or rarer items.

Tappables		Resources
	Grass	Gravel, dirt, coarse dirt, flowers, red mushrooms, ferns, jungle saplings, acacia saplings, grass, wheat seeds, pumpkins, pumpkin seeds, cocoa beans, jumbo rabbits, vested rabbits, and melon golems.
	Pond	The same as the regular grass tappable, plus clay, salmon, muddy foot rabbits, and glow squid.

Tappables   Resources

	Stone	Stone, andesite, cobblestone, diorite, granite, brown mushrooms, flint, sand, redstone, skeleton, furnace golem, skeleton wolf.
	Chest	Adventure crystals, oak planks, oak stairs, oak slabs, oak doors, oak fence, oak gate, oak pressure plate, torches, polished andesite (blocks, slabs, or stairs), polished diorite (blocks, slabs, or stairs), polished granite (blocks, slabs, or stairs), stone brick blocks, cobblestone walls, powered rails, rails, redstone lamp, redstone repeater, redstone torch, noteblock, minecarts, iron bars, iron bucket, bucket of mud, lever, cobweb, ink sacs, beetroot seeds, bonemeal, flowerpot, clay, clay blocks, glass blocks, TNT.
	Sheep	Sheep, horned sheep, flecked sheep, rocky sheep.

Tappables	Resources
Cow	Cow, wooly cow, ashen cow, sunset cow, moobloom
Chicken	Chicken, feather, egg, stormy chicken, amber chicken, cluckshroom
Pig	Pig, spotted pig, muddy pig, pale pig, piebald pig
Oak	Oak logs and saplings

	Tappables	Resources
	Birch	Birch logs and saplings
	Spruce	Spruce logs and saplings

Some resources (and animals, or mobs) are much rarer than others, and every type of resource has a rarity level: Common, Uncommon, Rare, Epic, and Legendary. Any tappable is more likely to have common and uncommon resources, and legendary items are usually only found in Adventures or by crafting. Each rarity level has a color associated with it too:

- **Common:** Gray
- **Uncommon:** Green
- **Rare:** Blue
- **Epic:** Purple
- **Legendary:** Gold

Tappable Rarity

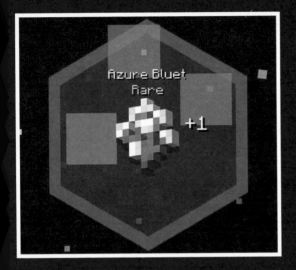

Azure Bluet
Rare

+1

When you are clicking a tappable, a hexagon border will show, and the color of that hexagon reveals the highest level of rarity of its resources. So when you tap a Grass tappable that has an Rare level azalea flower, the hexagon that shows when you tap is colored blue. (You also have to tap for longer with rarer tappables —five taps for an epic tappable compared to three for rare and uncommon tappables.)

As you collect tappables, you'll also collect experience. The amount of experience points depends on the resource or animal (mob). You'll only net 4 experience points (XP) for an Epic rarity level spruce sapling from a spruce tree, but nabbing a rocky sheep from a sheep tappable will net you 60 XPs. In general, collecting mobs from your World Map bring in the most experience out of tappables. To further boost your experience points, complete challenges and play adventures.

Inventory

As you collect from tappables, your resources will automatically transfer to your inventory. Click the chest on the World Map screen to access your inventory. At the very bottom is a row of seven boxes which form your hotbar. This is the first place that resources are transferred to and it shows up for easy access in the Buildplate and Adventure screens, although you don't see it in the World Map screen. Your main inventory, the grid above your hotbar, is filled once your hotbar is full. You can scroll through the inventory, sort it, or select a category view. You can also transfer items back and forth between your main inventory and your hotbar.

Your Inventory and Hotbar

(A) VIEW YOUR INVENTORY BY CATEGORY. FROM LEFT TO RIGHT
All, Mobs, Construction, Nature, Equipment, Items

(B) SORT YOUR INVENTORY

(C) SEE DETAILS ABOUT AN ITEM

(D) MAIN INVENTORY

(E) AMOUNT OF ITEMS

(F) HOTBAR USED IN BUILDPLATES AND ADVENTURES

(G) SEARCH FOR AN ITEM

To find out more about any object you have, click on it in your main inventory and then press the information ("I") button. Also notice the border around items in your inventory—the color shows you its rarity level.

Moving Stuff Around

To transfer an item from your hotbar to the main inventory, click on the hotbar item and then on any square in your inventory.

To move something from your main inventory to your hotbar, click on the main inventory item and then on an empty square in the hotbar.

To swap two items between your hotbar and your main inventory, click on the main inventory item and then on the item in your hotbar. You can also click on two items in your hotbar to swap their positions.

Stack Size

In your main inventory, all items are stacked in one square—you can have 1000 oak logs, and they will just take up one square. Your hotbar works differently however. The maximum amount most items can stack up to in one square in your hotbar is 64, but there is a big restriction on some very important items. Tools and weapons and buckets can only be stored in your hotbar one item at a time.

Blocks and Items and Entities and Mobs

The main categories of "stuff" in Minecraft are blocks and items. Blocks are the cubes that the Minecraft world is made of: blocks of grass and dirt, blocks of stone, blocks of logs and planks. Blocks can be placed in the world and on top of one another, and except for some rare blocks, you can remove a block from a column of placed blocks and the top blocks will stay in place. There are just a few blocks—sand and gravel—that have "gravity" and will fall to land on the nearest block below them.

The non-blocky stuff in Minecraft are typically called "items." These include things that you hold and cannot place on another block, like tools and weapons, and non-block-shaped stuff that can be placed in the world, like a flowerpot. Items that can be placed, like the flowerpot, still are confined to taking up just one block's space.

Other types of Minecraft objects include entities and mobs. Entities are any moving object. Entities include minecarts, arrows, lit (primed) TNT, throwable snowballs, mobs, and players. Mobs are the most complex entities ("mob" stands for "mobile") as most have a complicated programming for spawning, moving around, attacking, dying, and more. Mobs are the "animals" of minecraft.

Blocks, Items, and Entities

The stuff of Minecraft is often categorized as blocks (stuff that can be placed, like a block), items (things that are held or used), and entities (objects that can move).

Crafting

Crafting lets you make new stuff out of your resources. For example, if you have some oak logs in your inventory, you can use these to make oak planks, sticks, and other stuff. If you have sticks and planks, you can make fences and gates.

To open up the crafting interface, click the Make Stuff button on the World Map screen, then click the Crafting button. The Crafting interface will let you know what kinds of stuff you can craft, given your resources. It also shows you how many of an item you can craft, and the outline of any item shows you its rarity level. Crafting does take time, and rarer resources can take quite a bit longer than say, simple sticks. If you are gearing up for playing an adventure, craft essential weapons ahead of time.

To craft an item, click on the item in the grid and then click an open crafting slot at the bottom of the screen. Alternately, double-click any item. The crafting screen that pops up will show you how long your crafting session will take.

The Crafting Screen

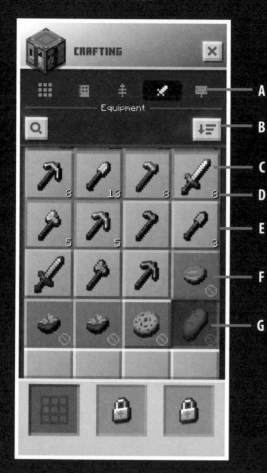

(A) VIEW RECIPES BY CATEGORY

(B) SORT RECIPES

(C) ITEMS YOU CAN CRAFT (GRAY BACKGROUND)
Click an item to view how many of that item you already have.

(D) NUMBER OF THE ITEM THAT YOU HAVE ENOUGH MATERIALS TO CRAFT

(E) BORDER COLOR SHOWS RARITY OF ITEM

(F) NOT ENOUGH MATERIALS TO CRAFT (RED BACKGROUND)

(G) NONE OF THE MATERIALS TO CRAFT (DARK GRAY BACKGROUND)

(H) CRAFTING SLOTS
Only one is unlocked

Sorting Crafting Recipes

To find the quickest recipes to craft, click Duration. Click here to show all recipes, including recipes you don't have the materials for.

In the Sort by menu, click "Show all recipes" to show recipes for stuff that you are missing resources for. This makes it much easier to see stuff you can make and what you need to make it.

Crafted Objects

While the Crafting interface will show you what's available to make from your resources, there are a few items and blocks you can craft that aren't so obvious, like:

- **Dye** (from flowers, cactus, bonemeal, cocoa beans, ink sacs)
- **Bricks** (from clay)
- **Minecarts** (from iron ingots)
- **Rails** (iron ingots and sticks)
- **Activator Rails** (iron ingots, sticks, and redstone torches)
- **Powered Rails** (from gold ingots, sticks, redstone)
- **Detector Rails** (from iron ingots, stone pressure plate, and redstone)
- **Glass Panes** (from glass blocks)
- **Dyed Terracotta** (from terracotta and dye)
- **Beds** (from wool or dyed wool and wood planks)
- **Mossy Cobblestone** (from vines and cobblestone)
- **Mossy Stone Bricks** (from stone bricks and vines)
- **Dyed Wool** (from dye and wool)
- **Paper** (from sugarcane)
- **Books** (from paper and leather)
- **Bookshelves** (from books and wood planks)
- **Tripwire hooks** (from iron ingots, sticks, and wood planks)
- **Redstone repeaters** (from redstone torches, redstone, and stone)
- **Hay Blocks** (from wheat)

Crafted Objects

Tools and weapons must be crafted. Some weapons are must-haves in order to succeed in Adventures: Swords and pickaxes. Tools and weapons can be made out of different materials, and the material determines how fast the tool works and how long it lasts. In increasing effectiveness, tool materials are wood, stone, gold, iron, and diamond. Gold is an expensive material that isn't very durable and is usually a poor choice for a tool or weapon. An iron pick or higher is needed to mine gold ore and diamonds.

Tools and Weapons of Minecraft

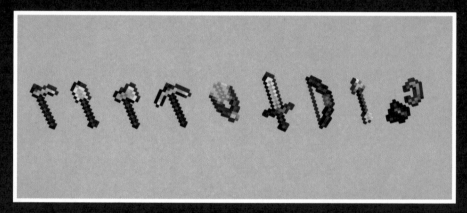

From left to right: hoe, shovel, axe, pickaxe, shears, sword, bow, arrow, flint and steel.

Smelting

Smelting (cooking in a furnace) is another way to get new and different resources. As with Crafting, it takes time to smelt a resource, and rarer items take longer. If you are playing a lot of adventures, you'll want to make sure you are on top of smelting iron ores for weapons and cooking food that will restore your health. There are also some decorative blocks that you can only get through smelting, like glass blocks and terracotta. Terracotta comes from smelting clay blocks, and patterned Glazed Terracotta is made by smelting colored (dyed) terracotta.

Tools and Weapons of Minecraft

(A) VIEW SMELTING RECIPES BY CATEGORY

(B) SORT RECIPES
(Click here to open the sorting panel and enable all recipes)

(C) SMELTED ITEMS YOU CAN MAKE
(Gray background)

(D) NUMBER OF THE ITEM YOU CAN SMELT TO MAKE

(E) SMELTING RECIPES YOU DON'T HAVE THE RESOURCES FOR

(F) FURNACE SLOTS
(Two are locked.)

To open the Smelting interface, click Make Stuff on the main World Map screen, then click Smelting. The Smelting screen is organized like the Crafting screen and shows you the "recipes" for items you're able to create by smelting. To create one of these, click on the item's square and then tap on the open furnace at the bottom of the screen. This will open up the furnace screen, and you'll see the item to be smelted at the top square and the fuel in the bottom square. To add or change the fuel, click on the fuel's square and select a fuel source and amount from the fuel screen.

The Furnace Screen

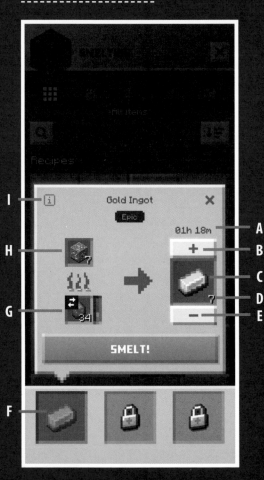

(A) TIME IT WILL TAKE TO COMPLETE SMELTING

(B) CLICK TO SMELT MORE ITEMS

(C) ITEM CREATED BY SMELTING

(D) NUMBER OF SMELTED ITEMS

(E) CLICK HERE TO SMELT FEWER ITEMS
(Clicking below 1 will set the amount to a full stack, usually 64.)

(F) FURNACE SLOT TO BE USED

(G) FUEL AND AMOUNT OF FUEL TO BE USED
(Click to change the fuel type.)

(H) RESOURCE ITEMS THAT WILL BE SMELTED

(I) CLICK FOR MORE INFORMATION ABOUT THE SMELTED ITEM

You can use wood logs, planks, and other wood items as fuel, as well as coal, charcoal, or a bucket of lava. Some fuel types will smelt for longer times, and some fuel types are harder to get than others. Coal is hard to come by because coal ore must be gathered from adventures. An easy way to keep plenty of cheap fuel on hand is to smelt wood logs using wood planks as a fuel source. That makes lots of charcoal for your smelting tasks.

Maker Multitasking

You don't have to stay on the crafting or smelting screens once you've set something up for crafting or smelting. Go about your tasks collecting or adventuring or building and you'll be notified when your items are ready.

CHAPTER 3

MEETING THE MOBS

Many of the mobs in Minecraft Earth are also in the classic Minecraft Game. But some of these species are entirely unique to Minecraft Earth! The Development team at Mojang will continue to add more unusual, crazy, and fierce mobs, variants, and hybrids for your collecting and battling pleasure!

Mobs can be passive (they won't attack you), neutral (they'll usually only fight back if you attack them), or hostile (they attack on sight!). It's pretty easy to figure out what's what. If a mob belongs in a peaceful country or farm setting, you're likely safe. If it is scary, creepy or weird, probably not. If it's holding a bow or sword, duck for cover!

MOBS OF MOBS

Outside of the game, "mob" means a big rowdy crowd. But in-game, the word "Mob" is shorthand for "mobile" entity and is used for any type of creature—from peaceful cows to the hostile skeleton. Even you are a mob—a playable one!

When you kill a mob, it disappears in a puff of smoke and usually (but not always) leaves something useful in its place, a "drop." A chicken will drop some raw chicken you can cook for food, and a creeper will drop a little gunpowder, useful for making explosive TNT!

Different mobs have different health levels, and the more health, the more difficult to kill. As you'd suspect, the larger and fiercer mobs have the most health levels. Health is measured in points, and shown in the UI as hearts: 2 health points equals 1 heart.

Collecting mobs from a tappable will also bring you valuable experience points and they're one of the best ways, outside of challenges and adventures, to boost your experience level.

Passive Mobs

Amber Chicken

A Minecraft Earth original. Just like a regular chicken, but amber!

Health: 4
Drops: Raw chicken, feathers, eggs
Found in: Chicken tappables

Ashen Cow

Unique to Minecraft Earth, this is a variant of the classic Minecraft cow.

Health: 10
Drops: Raw beef, leather
Found in: Cow tappables

Chicken

Unlike most mobs that are affected by gravity and can take fall damage, chickens slowly flutter down from a height. They also produce eggs occasionally. Minecraft Earth chicken variants include the Amber Chicken, the Stormy Chicken, and the Cluckshroom.

Health: 4
Drops: Raw Chicken, Feathers, Eggs
Found in: Chicken tappables, Buildplates, Adventures

Cluckshroom

The cluckshroom is a chicken/mushroom hybrid creature. Unlike the ordinary chicken, the cluckshroom prefers the dark, and will leave a trail of mushrooms as it meanders about.

Health: 4
Drops: Raw Chicken, Feathers
Found in: Chicken tappables, Buildplates, Adventures

Cow

If you click it with a bucket in your hand, you'll get a bucket of milk. (In regular Minecraft, you drink milk to remove any potion effects, good or bad, and this may be an upcoming feature in Minecraft Earth.) The beef it drops can be cooked in a furnace for one of the best foods in the game, cooked beef.

Variants: Wooly Cow, Ashen Cow, Sunset Cow
Health: 10
Drops: Beef, leather
Found in: Cow tappables, Buildplates, Adventures

Flecked Sheep

This wooly coated sheep variant will provide you with all your brown wool needs!

Health: 10
Drops: Raw mutton, wool
Found in: Sheep tappables

Glow Squid

It's a squid and it glows in the dark! You'll want to place this unique Minecraft Earth mob in a pond.

Health: 10
Drops: Ink sacs
Found in: Grassy Pond tappables

Jumbo Rabbit

The Jumbo Rabbit is just a really big rabbit!

Health: 3
Drops: Raw rabbit, rabbit hide, and (rarely) rabbit's foot
Found in: Grass tappables, buildplates

Mob of Me

The Mob of Me is a unique mob based on you! When you place it, it will take on your skin.

Health: 20
Drops: None
Found in: Chest tappable, buildplates

Moobloom

The Moobloom is a rare hybrid of the classic Minecraft cow and . . . a buttercup! As it ambles around it will leave a trail of sunny buttercups in its path.

Health: 10
Drops: Beef, leather
Found in: Cow tappables, buildplates

Muddy Pig

Unique to Minecraft Earth, this pig will skip to any nearby muddy hole to romp around. See Pig for stats.

Health: 10
Drops: Ink sacs
Found in: Pig tappables, buildplates, adventures

Muddy Rabbit

This rabbit variant is a fan of muddy pools, as evidenced by its muddy paws.

Health: 3
Drops: Raw rabbit, rabbit hide, rarely a rabbit's foot
Found in: Grass/Pond tappables

Ocelots

Ocelots are one of the natural inhabitants of the Jungle biome. They're very shy, unless you are a chicken and there for a tasty target. In other words, keep your chickens separate from your ocelots!

Health: 10
Drops: none
Found in: Buildplates

Pale Pig

This pig is a very light pink version of the traditional Minecraft Pig.

Health: 10
Drops: Raw pork
Found in: Pig tappables

Parrot

Parrots are the second mob unique to the Jungle biome, along with ocelots. Don't feed them cookies!

Health: 6
Drops: Feathers
Found in: Buildplates

Piebald Pig

"Piebald" means colored with odd splotches of two colors, often black and white. This Piebald pig has orangey brown splotches.

Health: 10
Drops: Raw pork
Found in: Pig tappables

Pig

In the main Minecraft game, pigs can actually be saddled and ridden with a carrot on a stick!

Health: 10
Drops: Raw pork
Found in: Pig tappables, Buildplates, Adventures

Rabbit

The easiest way to find this sand-colored rabbit is to download one of the desert-themed buildplates.

Health: 3
Drops: Raw rabbit, rabbit hide
Found in: Buildplates

Rocky Sheep

This Minecraft Earth variant of the classic sheep mob has a blocky brown pattern that would provide effective camouflage in a rocky road vanilla sundae.

Health: 10
Drops: Raw mutton, wool
Found in: Sheep tappables

Salmon

Salmon make for a colorful addition to your pond as well as a tasty meal.

Health: 3
Drops: Raw salmon, rarely bones
Found in: Grass (Pond) tappables

Sheep

The classic Minecraft sheep can be shorn with shears for its wool. It will need to eat a bit of grass in order to grow more wool.

Health: 8
Drops: Raw mutton, wool
Found in: Sheep tappables, buildplates, adventures

Spotted Pig

The Spotted Pig is just like a regular pig, jus with spots of black!

Health: 10
Drops: Raw pork
Found in: Pig tappables

Stormy Chicken

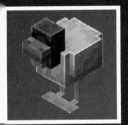

This chicken is colored with the hues of a thunder storm: gray and black.

Health: 4
Drops: Raw chicken, feathers, eggs
Found in: Chicken tappables

Sunset Cow

The sunset cow is a colorful variant of the classic Minecraft cow.

Health: 10
Drops: Raw beef, leather
Found in: Cow tappables

Tropical Fish

The orange and white striped tropical fish resembles a real world clownfish. Unlike other Minecraft fish, you cannot smelt it for a quick meal.

Health: 3
Drops: Clownfish, rarely bones
Found in: Tropical Slime (use a bucket)

Vested Rabbit

Is this a gray rabbit with a white vest or a white rabbit with gray trousers?

Health: 3
Drops: Raw rabbit, rabbit hide, rarely a rabbit's foot
Found in: Grass/Pond tappables.

Woolly Cow

This relative of the classic Minecraft cow comes from the cold biome of the Ice plains. Use shears on it to get some warm brown wool.

Health: 10
Drops: Raw beef, leather
Found in: Cow tappable

Neutral Mobs

Furnace Golem

The rare furnace golem is your defender, attacking hostile mobs with powerful arms and a fiery blast. That said, stay on its good side!

Health: 100
Drops: Coal, iron nuggets
Found in: Stone tappables

Golems Good

The idea of a golem comes from Jewish folklore and refers to a humanlike figure that is made from clay and then brought to life to perform tasks for its creator. In many stories, the golem turns against its creator. In Minecraft, a golem is also seen as a "created" creature that attacks hostiles to protect others. The main Minecraft game has two different golems, an Iron golem and a smaller Snow golem with a pumpkin head that shoots snowballs.

Horned Sheep

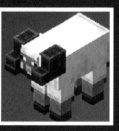

Unlike its tamer sheep cousin, the horned sheep will fight back if provoked. Don't get too close to it!

Health: 8
Drops: Wool, mutton, horn
Found in: Sheep tappables

Melon Golem

The Melon Golem is a snow person with a melon head and little stick arms. (Its counterpart in the main Minecraft game has a pumpkin for a head.) Like the Furnace golem, it will attack hostile mobs on site with its special attack—spitting melon seeds at them!

Health: 4
Drops: Melon slices
Found in: Grass tappables

Jolly Llama

The Jolly Llama, a llama festooned in holiday gear, made a brief appearance as part of a 2019 limited buildplate during the winter holidays! It may make more seasonal reappearances, so keep an eye out for new mobs to appear at special occasions. Note: Llamas in Minecraft are neutral—if you provoke them, they'll spit at you and it will hurt. Rumors have it that the Jolly Llama is especially fond of eating ferns . . .

Polar Bear

The Polar Bear is an inhabitant of Minecraft's icy biomes and is peaceful unless its young are in danger.

Health: 30
Drops: Raw fish, raw salmon
Found in: Buildplates

Hostile Mobs

Bone Spider

This Minecraft Earth spider-skeleton hybrid is the worst of the spiders! It has extra health so is especially difficult to kill. It will summon other spiders to help it attack you.

Health: 32
Drops: String, bones, bonemeal
Found in: Adventure chests

Creeper

The creeper has become the face of Minecraft, with its iconic mottled green skin and sizzling hiss as it approaches. If they get too close to you, they'll explode!

Health: 20
Drops: Gunpowder:
Found in: Adventures, rarely in Grass (Pond) tappables

From Whence the Creeper?

The Creeper was born from a mistake, when one of the Minecraft developers was working on a pig, and reversed the length of its height and width.

Skeleton

The classic Minecraft skeleton is equipped with a bow and limitless arrows which it will shoot at you every few seconds with deadly accuracy.

Health: 10
Drops: Arrows, bones
Found in: Adventures, rarely in Stone tappables

Skeleton Wolf

This dangerous hybrid skeleton wolf of Minecraft Earth is rumored to make nearby skeletons even more powerful.

Health: 10
Drops: Bones
Found in: Stone tappable

Spider

The scariest thing about spiders is that they can climb up vertical surfaces to attack you.

Health: 16
Drops: String
Found in: Adventures, rarely in Oak tree tappables

Tropical Slime

This Minecraft Earth bouncing block of goo can pack a punch. But if you click it with a bucket, you'll grab the tropical fish that live inside it and vanquish the slime.

Health: 16
Drops: Tropical fish
Found in: Grassy Pond tappables

Zombie

Zombies will hurt you if they get close, so kill them before they kill you! (Ever notice how the Minecraft zombies are wearing the same clothes as the original player character Steve?)

Health: 20
Drops: Zombie flesh, more rarely iron ingots and carrots
Found in: Adventures, Adventure Chests

CHAPTER 4

BUILDPLATES

Buildplates are your creative outlet in Minecraft Earth. They're there for you to dismantle for resources, create buildings, farms, castles, rollercoasters, and more. They are a Virtual Reality square section of Minecraft that you can place in your world (as seen through your smartphone) and modify to your heart's content.

The Buildplates Screen

(A) AVAILABLE BUILDPLATES TO PLAY

(B) CLICK TO JOIN OR ADD A FRIEND

(C) CLICK TO BUY MORE BUILDPLATES FOR RUBIES

(D) BUILDPLATE INFORMATION: LAST PLACED, SIZE, AND DAY/NIGHT

(E) CLICK TO PLAY IN BUILD MODE

(F) CLICK TO PLAY IN PLAY (FULL-SIZE) MODE

(G) CLICK TO SEND A COPY OF YOUR BUILDPLATE TO A FRIEND

There are both free and buyable buildplates in the game. Build-plates are all square and range in size from 8x8 blocks (width and length) to 32x32 blocks. Bigger isn't always better though – build-plates in Build mode are fit into the same area regardless of size, so the actual blocks in a 32x32 block buildplate are smaller and can be harder to interact with than in an 8x8 buildplate (It can be easier to work with a 32x32 buildplate if it is placed on a table you can be closer to.) Buildplates include several levels of below ground level blocks, and can be built up to 221 blocks high. Buildplates also come as either Nighttime or Daytime.

Buildplate Sizes and Times Compared

The larger the buildplate size, the smaller the blocks will be in Build mode. Left, an 8x8 daytime buildplate; right, a 16x16 nighttime buildplate.

Buildplates also come with a specified biome and time of day (either night or day). Biomes are a key feature of the natural environment in the main Minecraft game, and different biomes have different crea-tures, trees, flowers, and landscaping. The grass colors in different biomes are slightly different greens and the water colors in different ocean biomes are different as well. Biomes also figure into build-plates as well, and each buildplate is set in one of the Minecraft. The biomes you'll find on buildplates include Desert, Jungle, Plains, Snowy Tundra, Forest, and the Dark Forest (with dark oaks and giant mush-rooms). Other original-game Minecraft biomes are: Savanna (with acacia trees), River, Ocean, Forest, Taiga (with spruce trees), Moun-tains, Swamp (with vine-covered swamp oaks), and Birch Forest.

The creative builds by the game developers are delightful, but once you start dismantling a buildplate for resources and making your own builds, the original creation will be gone. Essentially, you are buying the plate and its size and biome and night/day setting from the store and not really the build itself, unless you decide not to use the plate for its resources. Buying Store-only buildplates can also be pretty pricey—some of the bigger ones cost 375 (just under $20) to 500 rubies (about $25), more than the cost of some entire games! You may want to start off a newly acquired buildplate by playing with it in real life size and in interact mode so you can appreciate it before you demolish it!

Resource Gathering

It is easy to tap blocks and "hard" items like fences and gates from a buildplate by tapping on them in Pickup mode. You can tap on mobs in the same way to store them in your inventory. It is a little tricker to get the liquids from a buildplate—you'll need to craft a bucket first (with 3 iron ingots) or be gifted a bucket from a chest tappable. To get mud, water, or lava from a buildplate, just click on that block with a bucket.

Bedrock Bottom

At the bottom of a buildplate (and at the outer edges and bottoms of Adventures) is a final level of a black and white block called bedrock. Bedrock is the "hardest" block in Minecraft—it's the one block that cannot be broken (except for some tricks in the regular Minecraft game) and is used as the bottom blocks of a world.

In Play mode, you can place your buildplate at "real life" size. This lets you walk around your build as if you are inside it, and is great for showing off to friends. However, while you can place and re-move blocks in play mode, any changes you make in this mode ar-en't saved. Your buildplate will remain the same as it was before you entered Play Mode.

Building on a Buildplate

(A) MORE BUTTON.
   Click here to close the
   session.
(B) PRECISION CURSOR LETS
   YOU SEE WHAT BLOCK YOU
   ARE AIMING AT
   To turn this on, click the
   More button
(C) MAIN INVENTORY BUTTON
(D) HOTBAR
(E) PICKUP MODE
(F) INTERACT MODE

Placing and Playing on a Buildplate

To get started with buildplates:

1. Click the Buildplate icon on the World Map screen.

2. The Buildplates screen will show you a selection of free build-plates. Some of these are locked, and will only unlock once you reach a specific experience level. On the Buildplate screen, select a buildplate by clicking "Build" under its image. The game will take a little time to prepare for setting up the buildplate. (If you want to play in Play Mode, click the arrow to the right of the Build button.)

3. Move your smartphone slowly over a fairly bright, flat surface, like a floor or a large flat coffee table. When the game recognizes your surface, you'll get a notice that you are "Ready to go" and see a big "Place" button. You can still move the plate a little bit now and even rotate it by swiping in a circular motion.

4. When you're happy with the buildplate's position, click Place.

5. The buildplate will "stick" to the surface, and you can move around it to see it from different angles on your device's screen. You can interact with your buildplate in Interact mode or Pickup mode. In Interact mode, you'll need tools to pick up most blocks, and hitting an animal will cause it damage. You can open doors and press buttons. You can also swipe in a circular motion be-neath the buildplate to rotate the buildplate. In Pickup mode, you need to just click on blocks to break them and have them whiz into your inventory. You can place blocks in either mode.

6. When you are ready to stop playing, click the More (3 dots) button at the top right of the screen and click on the Back to Map button.

The More Screen

A

B

C

D

E

F

(A) CLICK TO RETURN TO BUILDING SESSION
(B) CLICK TO FINISH BUILDING AND CLOSE THE BUILDPLATE
(C) CLICK TO REPOSITION THE BUILDPLATE
(D) TURN ON THE CURSOR
(E) CLICK FOR BETTER IMAGERY IN BRIGHT (SUNNY) CONDITIONS
(F) SHARE A TEMPORARY COPY OF YOUR BUILDPLATE WITH A LINK BY EMAIL OR SOCIAL MEDIA.

NO FLAT SURFACES?

Trouble finding the flat surface? The game will guide you a bit with placing surfaces, and will tell you when the area is too dark or you are moving your device too quickly. As you move your device, you may see small white diamond-like, sparkley icons that show the game is analyzing the surface. The surface doesn't need to be absolutely flat—a gravel path can work. The game does need "texture," a contrasty appearance with small light and dark patches, as this helps the application "see" the surface. If you are stuck trying to get the game to recognize your flat surface, you can try placing a thin, patterned cloth or a flattened newspaper spread on your floor.

Placing and Removing Blocks

To place blocks, select the block in your hotbar, so that its square is highlighted, and then position your cursor in the area you want to place that block. Then click! Make sure to click quickly, because holding down on the screen can result in spamming a bunch of blocks, on the buildplate. It is very easy to remove the blocks however, as you can just tap them (quickly again) in Pick-up mode. You can only place blocks that are in your hotbar, but you can easily add blocks to your hotbar by moving blocks from your main inventory to your hotbar.

Buildplate in Play Mode

In Play mode, things are much much bigger! You'll need a big space to play these, or you may be running into walls.

Play Mode

In Play mode, you can choose either Punch Mode or Interact mode. You'll need Interact mode for switching levers and pressing buttons and such and in this mode you need the right tool for any block breaking. In punch mode, you can "punch" or click repeatedly without a tool to break soft blocks like sand and wood, but you will still need the right tool for harder blocks.

The Right Tool for the Job

When you are playing in Interact mode in a buildplate or playing in an Adventure, you are playing a version of survival Minecraft in which you can only break some blocks with your hand. Other blocks you can only break with the appropriate tool:

- **Wood pick**: Hard blocks, such as stone, but no ore blocks.
- **Stone pick**: Coal ore and iron ore and anything a wood pick can break.
- **Iron pick**: Anything a stone pick can break as well as gold ore, redstone, and diamond.
- **Diamond pick**: Anything an iron pick can break as well as obsidian blocks.
- **Shovel**: "Soft" blocks: Dirt, sand, and gravel. Right-click a shovel on a grass block to create a path block.
- **Axe**: Trees, wooden blocks, and crafted wooden blocks, like fences. You also use an axe to right-click a log to "strip" it of its bark. This makes for an interesting building block—"stripped" logs.
- **Shears**: Cobwebs, to get cobwebs as a drop (they will otherwise drop string); vines, wool from sheep.
- **Hoe**: Right click on a grass block to create a farm block ready for planting.

You'll want to be in Interact mode if you are planning on using a specialized tool or block: If you want to switch a lever on a redstone contraption or use shears on a sheep.

Playing with Friends

You can share your buildplate with other players near you (right near you, like in the same room), and they can help you build. To do so, first set up your buildplate, then click the More button, and then click Invite Friend. You'll have to show the next screen to your friends so that they can scan the QR code on it. Similarly, if you want to join your friend's buildplate, once they've set up Invite Friend, you can then go to the Buildplates main screen and click on the QR button on the top menu. A screen appears with a placeholder to guide you in scanning your friend's QR code.

Playing with Friends

When you're inviting a friend to play on your buildplate, you'll be given a QR code (left) that they must scan with their own device (right). Your friend will need to match up the code and image on your screen with the outlines on theirs.

Sharing a Buildplate

You can share a copy of your buildplate with a remote friend by sending a link. Click the Share button beside a buildplate on the main Buildplate page. This will open up a page with contacts to send the link to and other ways and apps to share your buildplate and your hotbar. The buildplate you send will be a temporary "copy" of your build, so any changes the recipient makes won't be saved, and they won't get to keep any of the hotbar resources. It is nonetheless a great way to show off a build or explain how you made a contraption!

Sharing a Buildplate

When you share a link to a buildplate, you'll also send them your hotbar. It's all temporary though, your friend can't keep anything or change anything on your original buildplate.

Building Ideas

You're limited in the space you can build on with a buildplate, but often a restriction like this can make for great creative ideas. People are building tall towers and castles, farms, rollercoasters, and even fun challenges for friends to try with the Share function. (For example, can your friend get through a life-size mini-maze without dying to skeletons?). You can also use buildplates to store your lava and water, rather than keeping these in stacked buckets. It is also fun to use a buildplate to show off the rare blocks and mobs you've collected; just be sure to separate passive mobs and the mini-me from hostile mobs. Sometimes hostile mobs can attack and kill each other (this usually happens when one is aiming at you, and accidentally hits another mob that gets in the way).

Liquids

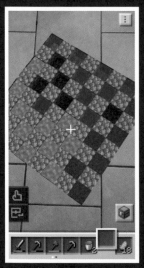

The "Flex" Buildplate

Some people are using buildplates and images of them to show all the rare loot and stuff they've collected, from diamonds and glazed terracotta to rare mobs.

CHAPTER 5

ADVENTURING

Adventuring is how you will get the best loot in the game (ores and diamonds), but for a price: the risk of losing your inventory by "dying" to mob battle. Each adventure is a special buildplate that you place and explore. But adventures don't have a "Pickup" mode—you'll be interacting with these worlds in much the same way you interact with worlds in the original Minecraft game. This means you'll need the right tool to break blocks, and using the wrong tool can mean it either takes a very long time to break or that it will just disappear after being broken: no resource given. You'll need a stone or iron pick to mine ore, a wood pick or better to mine stone and cobblestone, and a sword to fight mobs like spiders, skeletons, and creepers.

Adventure Builds

The above-ground builds in Adventures are often deceptively simple, like these four recreations of original adventures.

Adventure buildplates typically have a small "overground" build, perhaps a small farmhouse or even just a tree, and maybe some mobs wandering about. When you mine beneath their surface blocks, you'll find a cave or dungeon or other potentially lethal build. Some adventures will have no hostile mobs (typically the Level 1 or Common Crystal Adventures). The higher the level of the Adventure, the more mobs you can expect, along with a higher difficulty in killing them.

Limited Sight

It's almost impossible to see an entire adventure build on your screen; you'll need to move around and keep looking to investigate what's there.

There are two types of Adventures, the classic, original Adventures that appear on the map, and Crystal Adventures that you can play at home.

Original Adventures

The original outdoor adventures show on the World Map with a beacon—a column of light that spears the sky. You can't miss them! To play them, you do need to be fairly near to them. The radius for accessing one of these adventures is much smaller than the radius for tappables. This is because the game tries to choose safe public spaces, like parks, for adventure locations. Classic adventures only appear on the World Map for a certain amount of time, about seven minutes, before they disappear. Since they usually spawn in the same types of locations, you'll often find a new adventure spawning at or near the same location a few minutes after one disappears.

Outdoor Adventures

The original adventures you play outdoors in public spaces are shown with a beacon on your world map. You need to be within the blue radius to play them.

There are three types of original Adventures, Level 1 (easiest, usu-ally peaceful), Level 2 (some mobs), and Level 3 (most difficult and dangerous). The icon for the adventure on the World Map shows the level. The grassy mound with the oak tree is the lowest level; Level 2 has a birch tree and a skeleton, and the highest level has an icon with several skeletons, lava, iron bars, and a mob spawner.

To play a classic adventure, get close enough so that the blue circle shows up on your map and then move within this radius. Now you can click on the adventure, and press Play. You'll be prompted to play the adventure in the same way as a buildplate.

Adventures Screen

Choose a crystal from the bottom row and then click Activate to start your adventure.

Click here to invite a friend

Click for more information about the crystal

Adventure information: Time you'll have to complete it, the loot chest level (common to epic), and the size.

Your stored crystals—you can only have up to 3 crystals of a type at a time

Crystal Adventures

Crystal adventures are local adventures that you can play at your home or wherever you are; you don't need to travel to a public space. You'll need a crystal to play an adventure. There are five types of crystals, representing five difficulty levels of adventures: Common (Gray), Uncommon (Green), Rare (Blue), Epic (Purple), and Legendary (Gold). You can get Common crystals from Chest tappables and as a reward from challenges, and higher level crystals as rewards from playing adventures.

Unfortunately, you can only have 3 crystals of each type stored at a time. This means if you have 3 rare crystals, and receive a fourth rare crystal, that last crystal will be discarded. However, since you usually get a common crystal with every common adventure, you'll often be collecting more common crystals than you can store.

Each crystal adventure has a goal and when you reach it, you'll hear a majestic tune play. In addition, an adventure chest will appear with special loot. The goal may be simply to uncover specific blocks in the game, or to defeat all the mobs, or solve a puzzle, and goals increase in difficulty the rarer the adventure.

Playing a Crystal Adventure

To play a crystal adventure, highlight the crystal first and then click activate. You'll be prompted to place the adventure in the same way as a buildplate. However, crystal adventures are played "life size" and take a much bigger space. You'll want a fairly open space so that you can move around the edges of the adventure (about 4 meters square). With higher level adventures, with more mobs, you may want even more space so that you can move quickly away from firing skeletons!

Battery drain
Playing a buildplate or adventures can drain your battery, so keep an eye on your levels.

Once you've placed the buildplate, you are on a time limit—you have about 10 minutes to finish and reach the goal. When your time is running out, a red hourglass will appear at the top right of your screen. When time is up, the Adventure buildplate will disappear, and you'll be shown a screen with the loot you've acquired.

Adventure Time

There's a timer on an adventure that runs as soon as you've selected it. The hourglass at the top will show you how much time is left.

If you are playing a peaceful adventure (most Common Adventures are peaceful), you can go right ahead breaking blocks in the adventure build to reveal the underground build. The ores you want may be placed along the walls and floor, but very often they're hidden in corners and behind other blocks like stone, or behind and underneath water and lava flows. There aren't very many ores in an adventure, you'll often find between 2 and 6 ores of one to three different types.

Minecraft Ores

		Uses
	Coal	Mining coal ore drops coal. Use it as fuel for smelting and to make torches.
	Iron	For better weapons and tools. Smelting this ore creates iron ingots.
	Gold	For crafting some special resources, like powered rails. Can be used for tools, but has very low durability. Smelting this ore creates gold ingots.

Uses

	Diamond	For top tier weapons. Mining this ore drops diamonds.
	Lapis	No use at present, but used in the original game for enchanting. Mining this ore drops lapis.
	Redstone	For redstone contraptions crafting functional redstone objects. Mining this ore drops redstone dust.

You'll want to kill the hostiles off first before they get you, and killing any peaceful mobs loitering above ground prevents them from getting in your way. If you think there will be a lot of mobs, it can be easier to battle them if you only create only a small opening to the build beneath. A small opening limits their access to you. You can also place blocks to limit the opening, and move quickly back from the plate so that they cannot see you. Keep an eye out for adventures with gaping holes to the underground build, as these make it easy for mobs to spot and target you. Also watch out for stepped blocks leading down—mobs can climb one block at a time, and stepped blocks mean mobs can move up to attack you at ground level. Most mobs can't jump up a two-block height, so break or place blocks to stop mobs doing this. Some of the harder adventures come with hostile mobs spawned right on the ground by you, so make sure to look all around the adventure's above-ground build when you first place it.

Skeletons Near!

You can tell a mob is hidden but near if an icon of its face appears on your screen. The position of the icon (and an arrow) shows you approximately where it is.

The most damaging hostiles are skeletons, as they move fast and can inflict a lot of damage with very accurate bow shooting. Spiders can climb up walls, so they are the most likely hostile to find a way to come above ground to attack you. Zombies and creepers don't inflict ranged damage, so you can take a somewhat more leisurely approach to killing them. However, be warned that a creeper can blow up if it gets too near to you, and this can inflict very heavy damage.

Overall, battling in Minecraft Earth is tricky, especially when there are skeletons involved, or when mobs have access to ground level and you. Use your first diamonds for the strongest sword in the game.

Puzzle Adventures

Some adventures have puzzles that you must solve in order to receive the precious adventure chest of loot. Things that indicate there is a puzzle to solve include the presence of redstone elements like levers, redstone lamps, buttons, broken rails, and decorative blocks in noticeable patterns. Look out for broken patterns. A broken pattern may be four flowerpots arranged in a square, with only one flowerpot containing a flower, and other flowers planted elsewhere in the build. This can indicate the three other flowerpots need to be filled with a flower, and you'll need to figure out which flower goes where. Or there may be four redstone lamps, each on a different wall, and only one is lit up by a lever. In this case, you will be looking for missing levers to light up the other redstone lamps. Rails placed above ground may be the supplies you need to fix a short, broken railtrack beneath ground.

Puzzle Adventures

You'll probably have a puzzle adventure on hand if you spot rails, levers, buttons, or other redstone mechanisms.

Some adventures will have "cursed" blocks that you must re-move to stop hostile mobs from spawning. These are typical-ly unusual blocks that you can spot pretty easily. For example, one adventure has four glazed terracotta blocks that stand out, and you must collect these to stop skeletons from spawning. In general, always look out for "unusual" blocks that are different from most of the other blocks in the build.

Finishing an Adventure

You can leave an adventure before your time is up by clicking the More button and selecting "Back to Map". When you fin-ish any adventure, you'll get a screen that shows you the loot you've collected and experience you've gained.

You can't immediately load up another crystal, like the original adventures; once you've loaded an adventure buildplate it will persist for the full ten minutes. However, you can load a build-plate, and you'll be prompted to discard the adventure in order to continue. You can load the buildplate, leave, then load up a new crystal adventure.

Health and Food

When you play an adventure, you can take damage from hostile mobs like skeletons and zombies attacking you. When you take damage, your red health bar will decrease, and you can only replenish it by eating. To eat while you are in an adventure, highlight its icon in your hotbar and then click on its tooltip. You can eat outside of an adventure by clicking on a food item in your inventory, then pressing the Information (i) button, and then clicking Eat.

The foods of Minecraft aren't created equal and some restore more hunger/health points (HP) when you eat them. When you can, stock up on the top foods to take on an adventure.

Food		Source	Health Points
Golden Carrot		Craft a carrot with 8 golden nuggets	10 HP
Rabbit Stew		Craft cooked rabbit with a carrot, baked potato, wooden bowl, and any mushroom	8 HP

Food		Source	Health Points
Mushroom Stew		Craft with a red mushroom, brown mushroom, and a wooden bowl	8 HP
Cooked Porkchop		Cook raw pork in a furnace	7 HP
Cooked Beef		Cook the raw beef dropped from cows	6 HP
Cooked Mutton		Cook raw mutton in a furnace	6 HP

Food		Source	Health Points
Beetroot Soup		Craft with beets and a wooden bowl	6 HP
Bread		Craft from 3 wheat	4 HP
Cooked Cod		Cook raw cod in a furnace	4 HP
Cooked Salmon		Cook raw salmon in a furnace	4 HP

Food		Source	Health Points
Cooked Chicken		Cook raw chicken in a furnace	4 HP
Cooked Rabbit		Cook raw rabbit in a furnace	4 HP
Pumpkin Pie		Craft from a pumpkin, sugar, and an egg	4 HP
Baked Potato		Cook a potato in a furnace	4 HP

Food		Source	Health Points
Cookie		Craft from cocoa beans and wheat	4 HP

Adventure Supplies

There are a few essentials that you'll want to take on any adventure: A stone sword or better for battling and a pickaxe for mining ores. While you can make wooden tools and swords, they don't last very long. Even stone tools don't last that long, so have several stone pickaxes on hand for any adventure, if you don't have an iron pick. In addition, you must have a stone pickaxe in order to mine iron and coal, and to mine any higher level ores, like gold and diamond, you'll need an iron pickaxe. Where do you get the iron to make the better tools? From lower level adventures. The most important tool to upgrade first to iron is your pickaxe. There are so many blocks you can get from an adventure (once you've killed off the baddies), you can almost wear out a single brand-new iron pick with one adventure. Lastly, smelt your iron and craft your tools ahead of time, as there's no way to craft during an adventure.

The essential supplies for taking on an adventure are:

1. **Stone or better sword**: Swords can also break soft blocks like dirt, and especially cobwebs and tree leaves, very quickly, but this will lower their durability. Once you've upgraded your pickaxe to iron, your sword is next.

2. **Iron pickaxe or several stone pickaxes**

3. **Food**

4. **Axe for breaking wooden blocks**: (Your pick can break wooden blocks, but it takes much longer and wears out your valuable pick.)

Other supplies to consider are:

1. **Extra blocks**: You'll get blocks from breaking the top build and mining stone underground, but a stack of easy-to-break dirt can ensure you have plenty of blocks to remove water and lava, and stop mobs from seeing you.

2. **Empty bucket(s)**: Many adventures have water flowing or lava flowing, which makes it difficult to see which blocks are where. You can use a bucket to pick up water or lava source blocks that you can later use on your buildplates also. If you don't need to gather lava or water, you can also remove water and lava by placing a block on top of the source blocks.

3. **Bucket of lava**: One tactic to help rid an adventure cave of mobs is to drop some lava at its entrance. The lava will kill mobs while you can stay safe off to the side as it does its work. You may not want to use this in puzzle adventures or in builds that have wooden resources you need or don't want to burn! Also, if the dungeon contains TNT the lava will set it off.

4. **TNT and flint and steel**: Another tactic is to place a block of TNT in an adventure dungeon and set it off (prime it) to kill nearby mobs. To prime TNT, you'll need a tool called the "flint and steel" (crafted with a piece of flint and one iron ingot). A TNT explosion will also explode nearby blocks, which you can pick up. However, in a puzzle adventure, it could also break essential blocks, preventing you from achieving the adventure's goal.

5. **Shovel for breaking dirt**: This isn't as necessary as an axe, because dirt, sand, and gravel blocks can break pretty quickly with an axe or pick.

6. **Bow and arrows**: You can use a bow to attack hostile mobs, but a sword is much better. A sword has long range, like a bow, and a bow takes a little time to draw (load with an arrow) and doesn't do as much damage as a good iron sword. You also take up two inventory spaces as you need to bring arrows.

7. **A couple torches**: The adventures underground usually have torches or lamps or lava to light them up. However, it is possible to break an existing torch and not retrieve it or fill in lava, and then you are in the dark. If you haven't brought torches though, try to retrieve any broken torches so that you can replace them to light up the underground build. (If you are in the dark, your pickaxe will make a striking motion accompanied by a buzz on your device whenever your cursor passes over a mineable block, so it is possible to mine in the dark.)

SOURCE BLOCKS
Water and lava in Minecraft have a "source" block. A full block of water or lava that flows in each direction away from the source. You can only pick up the liquid by using a bucket on the central source block, but you can remove the source block and the flow by placing a block on the same space the source is on.

Adventure Chests

Every adventure build includes a Adventure Chest of valuable loot, often hidden under blocks. They emit sparkles though, and this can help to find them. These can contain rare or hard to get items and blocks like carrots, potatoes, and chiseled quartz blocks, along with ores, weapons and tools, adventure crystals, and even mobs you can place on your buildplates. There are three levels of adventure chests with increasing values of contained loot: Common, Uncommon, and Rare.

Common Adventure Chest

Look out for sparkles coming from behind blocks, as this can be the adventure chest you are looking for.

CHAPTER 6

BUILDING FARMS AND CONTRAPTIONS

In addition to building creatively on buildplates, you can also use them for functional reasons. You can use them for storing liquids like water, mud, and lava. Ordinarily, these are stored in buckets in your inventory, and you may want to use these empty buckets for adventuring. You can construct a special holding area on a buildplate for keeping liquids you aren't using elsewhere.

Animal Farming

Some animals can be used for getting other resources: If you have hundreds of chickens, you MAY want a place to—*ahem*—dispose of them in order to get raw chicken to cook into roast chicken. A moobloom on a grassy patch will leave buttercups for you to collect, and a cluckshroom on a stone patch that is sheltered from the sun will plant mushrooms. If you are mixing farm animals and farm crops on a buildplate, use a fence to stop animals from trampling your plants, and keep the rabbits away from the carrots!

Sheep Farm

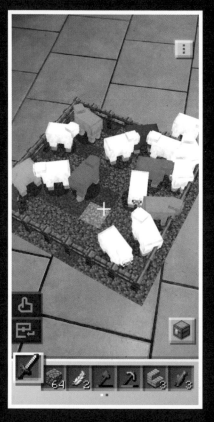

A farm of sheep will make it easy for you to gather wool, and if you color the sheep, colored wool.

Crop Farms

You can also set up crop farms and other plants on your build-plate. For a crop farm (carrot, potatoes, beetroots, wheat), you'll need to use a hoe on grass or dirt to create farmland. You should also make sure that each farmland block is watered by making sure it's within four blocks of a water block. An easy way to do this is to create a 9x9 square of farmland, with the central block water. Once you've prepared the land, plant whole carrots and potatoes, or beetroot or wheat seeds. There are several stages of plant growth before they are ready for harvesting. (The plants will only grow when your buildplate is in use.) To harvest, you can simply click on the plant, and you'll get 1 to 3 items of the grown plant. You'll then need to replant. Water will also break plants, and you can set up a contraption to release water that will flood your farmland whenever you want to.

Wheat, Beet, Melon and Pumpkin farm

Use a hoe on dirt to make farmland for growing crops and melons.

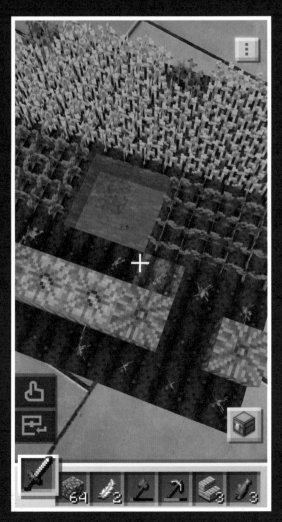

Melon and Pumpkin Farming

Melons and pumpkins grow a little differently from regular crops. Planting a seed on farmland (again, within four blocks of a water block) will grow a stalk. Then a grown melon or pumpkin will try to grow in a space next to the stalk. When you harvest the grown fruit, the stalk is left to continue to produce. This means when you set up the farm, ensure that there will be at least one free block of dirt, grass, or farmland next to each stalk.

Sugarcane Farm

Sugarcane is a resource you need to create sugar and paper. It needs to be planted on either dirt or sand next to a water block, and grows three blocks tall. To harvest it, just break the second block, which will make the second and third blocks of sugarcane drop. The bottom block of the sugarcane can be left in place to continue growing.

Cocoa Bean Farming

Cocoa beans are used for making cookies and creating brown dye that you can use on wool, beds, and in other recipes. You plant them on the sides of jungle oak logs.

Cactus Farming

You'll want to grow cactus if you need green dye. It does need to be planted on sand, with a block of space on each side. It doesn't need water. Like sugarcane, you can break the second block of the cactus to harvest so that you leave the bottom block in place to continue growing.

Multi-level Farm

To save on buildplates, combine your farms into a tower. Here cactus, sugarcane, and cocoa beans are on level 1, wheat on level 2, and some farm animals on the top level.

Seagrass

The only way to get seagrass, for planting in water, is to grow it by using (right-clicking) bonemeal underwater on sand or dirt.

Tree Farming

You can plant oak, birch, spruce, and acacia saplings on grass or dirt, with 2-3 blocks of space on each side, and they'll grow into full size trees. Tall jungle trees, giant spruces, and dark oaks need four saplings placed in a square to make a new tree.

Bonemeal

You can use bonemeal (from tappables or crafted from bones) to make some plants grow faster. Each bonemeal item clicked on the plant will give a chance of growth. This can be an expensive way to grow crops but it is helpful if you just need some extra carrots for a recipe. Cactus and sugarcane don't respond to bonemeal, but tree saplings and crops do. You can also use bonemeal on a patch of grass to grow grass and flowers.

Cobblestone Farming

In Minecraft, you can create cobblestone by letting a water flow and a lava flow meet in a specific way. You can mine the cobblestone block, and the two flows will replace it, giving you an infinite supply of cobblestone. To make this cobblestone magic happen, you create a cobblestone generator that makes sure that only the flows from the lava and water source blocks meet.

Cobblestone Generator

Build a trench four blocks long and one deep, then dig an extra block down at one of the middle blocks. Place a water source on the short end and a lava source on the longer end and this will create cobblestone next to the lava source block.

Dirt Farming

A dirt farm works in the same way as a cobblestone farm, except that the two sources are mud and lava. Again, you need to make sure that only the flows of these two sources meet.

Ice Farm

To farm ice, you'll need a snowy buildplate. In this, any water exposed to the sky will change to ice. Create a large, squarish pond. To fill it with water, place water source blocks in every other block space along two adjoining sides of the pond. This should result in the pond entirely filling up with water source blocks. Then, place blocks above the two adjoining sides of the pond. Covering them prevents them from turning into ice, and they will be able to flow to fill the pond again. Let the inside of the pond turn to ice, which you can harvest in Pickup mode.

Apples
You can only get apples from the leaves of an oak tree, and they are a rare drop. When you play an adventure that has an oak tree, try chopping down just the wood of the tree and let the leaves gradually despawn as you play the rest of the adventure. Some of the leaf blocks may drop an apple for you: extra loot!

Snow Farm

You can make a snow farm with melon golems, that are part snowpeople! When melon golems walk around, they leave a path of snow. To make a farm out of this function, you'll want to enclose a melon golem on a single block so that as you harvest its snow, it continues to create more.

Redstone Contraptions

Redstone in Minecraft is a kind of energy source, a bit like electricity. Redstone power can cause some special objects to perform an action. Redstone power comes from some objects, like levers, buttons, pressure plates, and redstone blocks. Objects that react include doors, gates, trapdoors, some rails. You can also carry a redstone power signal from a source to an object over several (up to 15) blocks by using a trail of redstone dust.

Redstone in the original Minecraft game is quite complex, and people have made incredible working contraptions with them. In Minecraft Earth, there are fewer redstone component blocks, but enough to make working railroads and automatic lighting and doors.

The redstone components in Minecraft Earth include:

Redstone dust: Carries a redstone signal up to 15 blocks.

Redstone block: Creates a redstone power signal.

Redstone torch: Creates a redstone power signal. If powered by another source, it will power off.

Repeater: Allows a redstone dust signal degraded by distance to return to full power. You can right-click to delay the signal from 1 to 4 redstone "ticks" (1/10th of a second). The repeater has a back and a front that the signal travels through, so you can also use them to make sure a signal is only traveling in one direction. Lastly, you can "lock" a repeater so that it doesn't change its output (whether on or off). To do this, you must power it by another repeater that faces its side. This last function is mostly useful in the more complicated contraptions.

Redstone lamp: Turns on with redstone power.

Lever: Creates redstone power.

Tripwire hook: When set up in pairs that are attached to each other by string, will create a redstone pulse when an entity passes through the string.

Doors, gates, and trapdoors: Will open with redstone power and close when the power is removed. Note: Iron doors and iron trapdoors only open with redstone signals.

Note Blocks: Produce a note when they receive a redstone signal. (The initial note it produces is F#. You can right-click the note block to raise the note a semitone, and you can raise it up to two octaves higher: F#, G, G#, A, A#, B, C, C#, D, D#, E, F, F#. You can create sequences of redstone-powered note blocks to create songs that will play on your buildplate.

Rails

To create a length of railway, place rails crafted from iron and sticks in a sequence on other blocks. You can join them in a circle for a complete circuit. Rails can be placed on one block-stepped inclines and made into corners. You'll need to use powered rails to make minecarts move around the track continually and also to make them go up any slopes. You'll want one powered rail for every 10 or so rails on a flat surface and more for going up slopes. You power a powered rail with a redstone power source, such as a flipped lever, redstone torch, or redstone block. However, you can power up to 17 powered rails in a row with a single power source. Powered rails can't be placed as corners.

Powered Rails

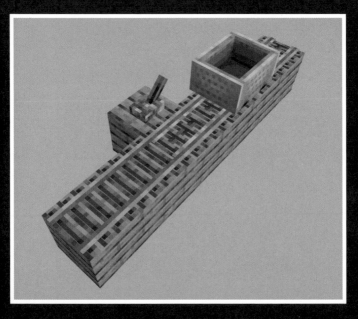

You can power up to 17 powered rails with a single lever, redstone torch, or redstone block.

Two other specialized types of rails that you can use in making contraptions are:

Activator rail: When powered, it will eject mobs from a minecart passing over it.

Detector rail: This produces a redstone power signal when a minecart passes over it

CHAPTER 7

UPPING YOUR GAME WITH CHALLENGES, BOOSTS, AND THE JOURNAL

Beyond tapping, collecting, building, and adventuring, you can greatly improve your experience and add to your loot by hunting down challenges to complete, completing your journal, and using boosts to help you in adventures and more.

Accessing Challenges

Click here for seasonal (2-week long) challenges

Green square shows you have new rewards from challenges

Click here for Career, Daily, and Tappables challenges

Challenges

Challenges are a great way to get to know the game and to collect more experience. More experience can sometimes grant you new game features. For example, new buildplates become available when you reach new experience levels. There are four types of challenges available. Three types of challenges are in the Challenges area: Career, Daily, and Tappables. A fourth set of challenges lie in the "Seasonal" challenges area.

Daily Goodies

When you first log in for the day to Minecraft Earth, you'll get goodies, such as rubies, diamonds, crystals, and a reminder of your daily challenges waiting for you. Remember, if you already have three crystals of one type, you can't receive any more until you empty a slot.

Career Challenges

Career challenges guide you through some of the main features of the game: collecting, crafting, smelting, and building. They are organized into stages that are locked until you complete the previous stage. Each stage has several tasks to complete in a certain order.

Career Challenges

Career challenges are sequential and are a great way to get more XP (experience points).

Career challenges (almost all of which have several steps) include:

- **Level Up**: Reach (Experience) Level 3

- **The Basics**: Planks—Collecting wood and crafting planks

- **The Basics**: Doors—Collecting wood and crafting doors

- **The Basics**: Torches—Collecting materials and crafting 4 torches

- **The Basics**: Glass—Collecting materials and making glass

- **The Basics**: Stairs—Collecting materials and crafting stairs

- **The Basics**: Tools—Collecting materials for crafting basic wood tools

- **Tools**: Stone Pickaxe—Collecting materials and crafting a stone pickaxe

- **Tools**: Stone Sword—Collecting materials and crafting a stone sword

- **Tools**: The Good Stuff—Mining iron ore and smelting it into ingots

TIP: Previously crafted, collected, and smelted items don't count—for each challenge you'll need to gather anew.

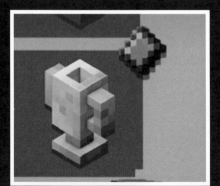

A tiny green square appears on your Challenges icon in your World Map when you have rewards to collect.

Daily Challenges

Daily challenges are changed every day—you'll complete one recurring daily challenge simply by logging into the game. The daily challenges are pretty easy and they usually include two collecting challenges and two buildplate challenges. You also get extra rewards the more challenges in a day you complete. Fulfilling all daily challenges can net you a cool 500 experience points and 5 rubies. Also note: once you place a block or mob on a buildplate for a Build Mode challenge, you can also remove it immediately; simply placing the item counts.

Daily challenges include:

• More Fuel (Make 4 charcoal)

• Adventurer (Play 1 Adventure)

Epic Tappable
If you need to collect any epic tappables, look for a spruce tree—the tallest of the trees. Spruce tree tappables often give you a spruce sapling, which counts as an epic item.

Crafting and Smelting Challenges
If you're given a challenge to smelt or craft any type of items, choose quickly craftable items like sticks (5 seconds to craft one stick) and quickly smeltable items (charcoal is much faster to smelt than iron ingots).

Challenge Buildplate

Dedicate one buildplate to fulfilling building challenges. For example, you could include an area to add blocks like oak logs, glass blocks, fences, doors, areas for harvesting crops and growing trees, and an animal pen for placing farm animals and shearing sheep. Or, like me, you could just add stuff randomly to your challenges plate when you need to!

Tappable Challenges

As you collect tappables in the World Map, you'll also be randomly given challenges under the "Tappable" category. You'll notice them when a rectangular slip of paper pops up on the World Map screen and jumps into the Challenges trophy icon. There are four levels of Tappable challenges: common, uncommon, rare, and epic. Higher levels are harder but offer more XP. If you don't want to do a particular challenge, you can click the trash icon next to the challenge's title.

Tappables Challenges

There are only three slots available for tappable challenges, so if you have all three slots filled with a new challenge, you won't receive any more tappable challenges until you empty up a slot. You can free up a slot by clicking the Trash icon by Tappable challenge though.

The color of the challenge title shows the challenge rarity level—gray for common, green for uncommon, blue for rare, and purple for epic.

Some sample Tappable challenges are:

- **Higher Ground**: Craft 5 stairs (25 XP)

- **Tickle time**: Collect 5 feathers from adventures (25 XP)

- **Adventure supplies**: Cook 10 food (40 XP)

- **Grill Time**: Cook 10 food (50 XP)

- **Moove Along**: Collect 1 moobloom (85 XP)

- **Scary sounds**: Defeat 3 bone spiders in adventures (150 XP)

- **Start a Zoo**: Place 15 mobs on a buildplate (150 XP)

Seasonal Challenges

Seasonal Challenges last two weeks and are based around a theme, like "Nature." Each season has a tree of challenges that unlock as you progress. Each challenge in the tree comes with a little loot, and if you finish the lot, you'll get more special rewards. You must select a challenge on this screen before completing it, in order to receive the rewards. You can switch between available challenges though.

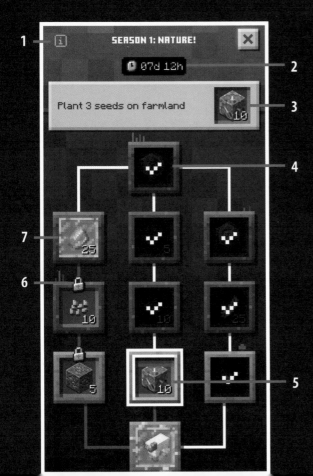

(1) CLICK HERE FOR MORE INFORMATION ABOUT THE SEASON AND REWARDS

(2) TIME LEFT TO COMPLETE THE ENTIRE CHALLENGE SET

(3) CURRENT CHALLENGE DESCRIPTION AND REWARDS

(4) COMPLETED CHALLENGE

(5) SELECTED CURRENT CHALLENGE

(6) LOCKED CHALLENGE

(7) UNSELECTED AVAILABLE CHALLENGE

The Journal

The Journal is your collectable tracker and it lists all the items you've collected. It doesn't give you any extra XP for collecting new items or blocks or mobs, but you do get the satisfaction of filling up the pages. Going through the journal pages will also show you all the stuff that is in Minecraft Earth, which isn't always obvious just from collecting and adventuring.

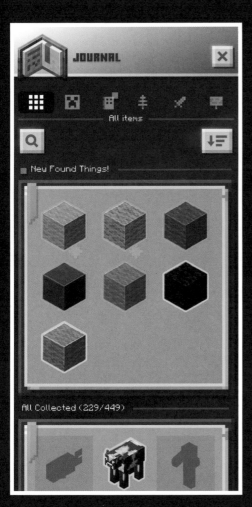

Your journal will show you any new items, blocks, and mobs you have found (or created from crafting or smelting), and you can see what is missing from your collection by the gray shadowed icons.

Boosts

Boosts are a way to change some game functions to your advantage—speeding up crafting time or giving you more attack damage for an adventure. There are two ways to get boosts: you can buy a boost using rubies from the Store or you can purchase a tiny action figure for about $5 from a real world toy store or department store. The action figures, called mini figures, are made by Mattel, and you can find them at popular stores like Target and Walmart. Each mini-figure will give you one type of boost that lasts for 10 minutes and can only be used once every 24 hours.

Click here to add a boost from a purchased mini figure

Regular boosts (non-mini figure) that you've purchased with rubies are highlighted here, along with how many you have. Click on one to see more information about what the boost does and how long it lasts.

In-game Boosts cover the same types of improvements but each boost (like increased attack damage) comes with three levels. Higher levels increases the amount of time the boost lasts and the power of the boost. However, you won't always need more time from a boost. If you are only planning on playing one adventure, an attacking boost that lasts 30 minutes will be mostly wasted.

Enabled Boosts

All your enabled boosts will appear below the side menu on your World Map screen. Click on it to see how much more time it has.

Note: If you are purchasing a Minecraft Earth mini figure for a boost, make sure the packaging calls it a Minecraft Boost, as there are plenty of non-boosting mini figures available.

Mini Figure Boosts

Figure	Boost
Healing Witch	10% increased health
Attacking Steve (x2)	25% increased attack damage
Hoarding Skeleton	Keep your backpack contents if you die
Snacking Rabbit (x2)	10% increased maximum health
Seeking Wolf	Map radius increased by 35 meters
Slowed Creeper	Gain 50% more experience points from adventures
Poison Enderman	25% increased attack damage
Defending Alex	25% stronger armor
Fishing Polar Bear	50% more filling food
Attacking Alex	25% increased attack damage
Regenerating Mooshroom	10% increase in maximum health
Smelting Blaze	10% faster smelting
Enraged Golum	25% stronger armor
Mining Creeper	25% increased mining speed
Undying Evoker	Keep your hotbar inventory if you die
Future Chicken Jockey	50% more experience when collecting mobs
Crafting Steve	100% faster crafting times
Crafting Villager	100% faster crafting times
Seeking Dolphin	35 meter increase in worldmap radius

In-game Boosts

Boost	Level 1 (10 minutes)	Level 2 (15 minutes)	Level 3 (30 minutes)
Radius	+35 meters	+53 meters	+70 meters
Mob XP	+50% XP	+ 75% XP	+ 100% XP
Crafting	+100% speed	+ 300% speed	+ 700% speed
Smelting	+10% speed	+20% speed	+ 30% speed
Keeper	Keep your hotbar if you die		
Hoarding	Keep your backback if you die		
Defense	+25% armor	+50% armor	+75% armor
Attack	25% attack strength	50% attack strength	100% attack strength
Mining	+25% mining speed	+50% mining speed	+100% mining speed
Adventure XP	+50% XP	+75% XP	+100% XP
Food	+50% food	+150% food	+300% food
Health	+10% health	+20% health	+30% health

How do the mini figures work?

The mini figures have an NFC (near-field communication) chip in them that sends a short-range wireless signal. The data that each figure has is unique. Your mobile device will have to be close to the figure (4 cm or less) to read the signal.

APPENDIX

MORE RESOURCES

Crafters Guide to Minecraft Earth

Craftersguide.stents.dev

This website is run by gamers who take an in-depth look at the code files of the game. It has detailed information about all of the resources you can find on buildplates and adventures, and includes layer by layer views of every adventure.

Official Minecraft Earth Discord

Discordapp.com/invite/minecraftearth

Discord is a popular chat application for Windows, Mac, Android, iOS and Linux, with thousands of different groups or "servers" hosting chats. You can download the app from discordapp.com or use it from its website at discordapp.com.

The official Minecraft Earth Discord is a fantastic resource and a moderated community hub for discussing all things Minecraft

Earth. It hosts live chats with the development team as well as regular build contests. You'll also find the latest game announcements and updates here (see "changelogs"), as well as discussion threads about general gameplay (minecraft earth), user builds, and areas to report bugs, give feedback, and ask for support. In the adventures section, you'll find loads of tips on solutions for adventure puzzles.

Official Minecraft Earth website

Minecraft.net/earth

This is the official Mojang website for the Minecraft Earth game. You can download the app from here and read the latest news about the game. You can contribute and vote on user feedback here at (Go to Feedback.minecraft.net, and select Minecraft Earth from the "Categories" menu) and report bugs and find support.

Official Minecraft Wiki

Minecraft.gamepedia.com

This is the official Minecraft wiki that includes in-depth, researched, user-contributed information on all the versions of Minecraft. Once there, search for "Minecraft Earth" to find more about the AR game.

What's a Wiki?

A wiki is a website for sharing knowledge that allows for many people to contribute to it and edit it. (The word "wiki" is a Hawaiian word for "fast".) One of the most popular wikis is Wikipedia (wikipedia.com), a massive wiki encyclopedia of general knowledge.

Play Minecraft Earth

Playminecraftearth.com

Play Minecraft Earth is an excellent unofficial news site and includes several step-by-step guides on troubleshooting technical difficulties such as License Errors, and compatibility issues.

Minecraft Earth Subreddit

reddit.com/r/Minecraft_Earth/

Reddit is a popular web-based bulletin board; discussion groups here are called subreddits. At the Minecraft Earth subreddit, you'll find gamers discussing features, problems, builds, and very useful information, but be forewarned that Reddit is not a site designed for children, and you will find plenty of grumpy people arguing at length here.